Manatees

written and photographed
by Frank Staub

└ Lerner Publications Company • Minneapolis, Minnesota

For the many animals that have suffered, because there are so many of us.

The author wishes to acknowledge Crystal River National Wildlife Refuge, Florida Power and Light Company, Homosassa Springs State Wildlife Park, Miami Seaquarium, David R. and Theresa L. Schrichte, and Mike Worwietz.

Photograph on page 17 is reproduced with the permission of the Florida Marine Research Institute, Florida Department of Natural Resources.

Thanks to our series consultant, Sharyn Fenwick, elementary science/math specialist. Mrs. Fenwick was the winner of the National Science Teachers Association 1991 Distinguished Teaching Award. She also was the recipient of the Presidential Award for Excellence in Math and Science Teaching, representing the state of Minnesota at the elementary level in 1992.

Early Bird Nature Books were conceptualized by Ruth Berman and designed by Steve Foley. Series editor is Joelle Goldman.

Website address: www.lernerbooks.com

Library of Congress Cataloging-in-Publication Data

Staub, Frank J.
    Manatees / written and photographed by Frank Staub.
        p. cm. — (Early bird nature books)
    Includes index.
    Summary: Describes the physical characteristics, behavior, habitat and endangered status of this gentle sea animal that is a relative of the elephant.
    ISBN 0-8225-3023-6 (alk. paper)
    1. Manatees—Juvenile literature.   I. Title.   II. Series.
QL737.S63S735   1998
599.55—dc21   97-33005

Manufactured in the United States of America
1 2 3 4 5 6 – SP – 03 02 01 00 99 98

Contents

CANADA

UNITED STATES

Manatees live in North America, South America, and Africa. The yellow areas show where manatees can be found in North America.

CENTRAL AMERICA

WEST INDIES

Be a Word Detective

Can you find these words as you read about the manatee's life? Be a detective and try to figure out what they mean. You can turn to the glossary on page 46 for help.

bulls	**extinct**	**nursing**
calves	**graze**	**snout**
cows	**herbivores**	**springs**
endangered	**mammals**	**streamlined**

Chapter 1

A manatee swims in a river in Florida. Manatees don't have legs. What do they have instead of legs?

Like Underwater Elephants

Fish swim in a quiet river in Florida. Plants sway in the water. In the distance, an animal appears. It is as big as a car. It is shaped like a submarine. Slowly, the animal swims closer. It is a manatee.

A manatee's head is small, and its neck is short. Its mouth and nose form a big snout. A manatee has a wide, round tail. Instead of legs, it has two flippers. At the end of each flipper are three or four fingernails. The animal's big body is covered with gray skin.

Adult manatees are 10 to 13 feet long. They weigh 1000 to 3000 pounds.

A manatee's snout is covered with whiskers.

A manatee's snout looks like a short, stubby elephant's trunk. The nails on the manatee's flippers look like an elephant's toenails. And the manatee's skin looks like an elephant's skin. That's because manatees are related to elephants.

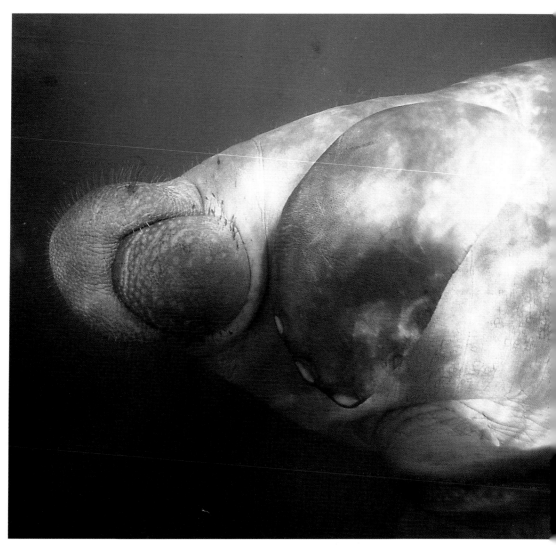

A manatee has three or four nails at the end of each flipper.

Millions of years ago, a kind of huge animal lived on earth. These animals walked on the land. They ate the leaves of trees.

Some of these animals began to live in the water. They ate water plants. A long time passed. Slowly, the animals changed. After millions of years, the animals began to look a bit like fish. They no longer had back legs.

Sometimes tiny green plants grow on a manatee's skin.

Manatees live in shallow water. Usually the water is less than 15 feet deep.

Instead of front legs they had flippers. And their tails were flat and round. The animals had become manatees.

The rest of the big animals stayed on the land. After millions of years, some of them had very long noses. Their noses were trunks that could reach leaves high in the treetops. These animals had become elephants.

Manatees may use their flippers to stay in one place or to move along the bottom.

A manatee doesn't need a trunk. A manatee lives in the water all its life. If a manatee wants something that is above it, it swims up. If it wants something that is below it, it swims down.

Manatees are streamlined. A streamlined body is smooth and round. A manatee's streamlined body moves through the water easily. The manatee's tail pushes it forward. Its flippers help it steer.

Manatees swim hundreds of miles each year. But they move slowly. They usually swim slower than 5 miles per hour. The fastest they ever go is about 15 miles per hour. If you could race a manatee on your bicycle, you might win.

When a manatee swims, its paddle-shaped tail pushes it forward.

Chapter 2

The kind of manatee that lives in North America is the West Indian manatee. Its scientific name is Trichechus manatus. *How many other kinds of manatees are there?*

Warm Waters

There are three species, or kinds, of manatees. They are the Amazonian manatee, the West African manatee, and the West Indian manatee. Amazonian manatees live in South America. West African manatees live along the western coast of Africa. And West Indian

manatees live in North America. Some West
Indian manatees live mainly in Florida. These
manatees are called Florida manatees.

All manatees need warm water to live in.
If the water around them is too cold, they get
sick. Then they stop eating and die.

The West Indian manatee is the largest kind of manatee.

In the spring, summer, and fall, Florida manatees live in shallow water along the ocean's shore. When winter comes, the ocean becomes cold. So the manatees leave the ocean. They move into rivers. In the rivers there are warm springs. Springs are places where water comes out of the ground.

A manatee rests in warm water from a spring. The water coming from the spring looks blue, and the cooler water from the river looks green.

16

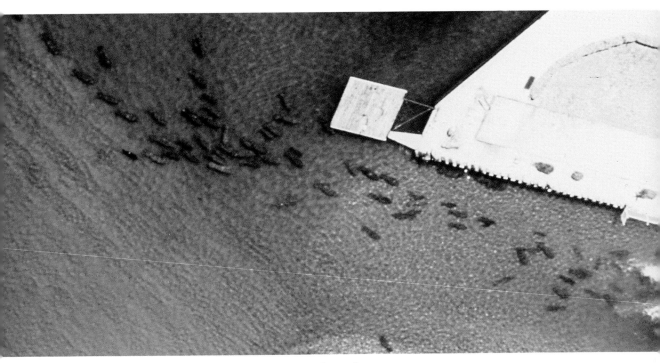

*Many manatees have gathered in the warm water
flowing out of a power plant.*

Many Florida manatees spend the winter
near power plants. Power plants are factories
that make electricity. Some power plants use
cold water from a river to keep their machines
cool. Then the power plants put the water back
into the river. When water comes out of a
power plant it is warm. It is just the way
manatees like it.

Chapter 3

This baby manatee is drinking its mother's milk. What do we call animals who drink milk?

The Sea Cow

Manatees live in the water. But they are not fish. They are mammals. Mammals are animals who drink their mother's milk.

All mammals have hair. Manatees don't have much hair, though. Manatees have so little hair that they look bald.

Fish can breathe underwater. But mammals cannot. When mammals swim, they must come to the surface to breathe air. Manatees often rest at the bottom of the water. But every few minutes, a resting manatee must rise to the surface to breathe.

A manatee can hold its breath for up to 20 minutes.
This manatee has come to the surface to breathe.

Manatees are herbivores (HUR-buh-vorz).
Herbivores are animals who eat mostly plants.
Manatees eat a lot. They eat up to 100 pounds
of plants each day.

A manatee uses its flippers to hold plants as it eats.

Some of the plants that manatees eat grow at the surface of the water. Others grow on the bottom.

Manatees spend six or seven hours every day eating water plants. They graze, like cows munching grass. Because manatees graze like cows, people sometimes call them "sea cows."

A manatee has big lips. The lips have tough pads. A manatee uses the pads to grab plants and pull them into its mouth.

A manatee's teeth are flat for grinding plants. Eating tough plants wears out a manatee's teeth. The worn-out teeth fall out.

This manatee's mouth is open. You can see its tough lip pads and some of its teeth.

Manatees use sand to clean their teeth. Sometimes manatees swallow sand. Sand helps a manatee's stomach grind up food.

But new teeth are always growing in the back of a manatee's mouth. They move forward when the front teeth fall out.

Sometimes bits of plants and dirt get stuck between a manatee's teeth. So after a manatee eats, it cleans its mouth. The manatee may use its flippers to clean its teeth. Or it may roll sand or gravel around in its mouth.

Chapter 4

Long ago, some people thought manatees were partly human. What did these people call creatures who were half fish and half human?

Songs of the Sirens

Manatees are in a group of mammals called the Sirenia. This name comes from stories of long ago. The stories told of creatures called sirens. The sirens were like mermaids. They were half fish and half woman.

In the stories, the sirens sang beautiful songs. Manatees don't sing. But they do squeak, chirp, and make other sounds.

Sound is important to manatees. A manatee can't see far in its dark underwater home. If the water is muddy, a manatee can't see at all. So it makes sounds to tell other manatees where it is.

The water around these manatees is cloudy. So the manatees can't see very far.

Sometimes manatees swim in groups. When manatees swim together, they touch each other often. They may touch noses, as if they are kissing. And sometimes they hold each other with their flippers.

Manatees spend much of their time alone. But sometimes groups of manatees swim together for a while.

Manatees seem to enjoy playing with other manatees.

Manatees like to play. They roll and twist and turn upside down. They play alone or with others. Sometimes they play follow the leader.

Chapter 5

A baby manatee swims beside its mother. How big is a newborn manatee?

Growing and Learning

Female manatees are called cows. Males are called bulls. And young manatees are calves.

A manatee cow has her first calf when she is about seven years old. After that, she gives birth about once every three years. Manatee cows usually have one calf at a time. But sometimes they have twins.

A newborn manatee is big. It is up to 4 feet long. And it weighs as much as 65 pounds. The chubby calf can swim when it is born. It knows how to go to the surface to breathe.

Manatee cows usually have only one calf at a time. But this manatee has twin calves.

Manatee cows take good care of their calves. If a calf loses its mother, another cow may adopt the calf.

At first, a calf drinks its mother's milk. This is called nursing. A calf can eat plants when it is only a few weeks old. But it nurses until it is almost two years old.

A manatee cow teaches her calf how to find food. She shows the calf where to find warm water in the winter.

A calf stays with its mother for two or three years. During that time, they are always together. When they are not touching, they call to one another.

A manatee calf drinks milk until it is almost fully grown. This calf is nearly as big as its mother.

Chapter 6

If a manatee is attacked, it can't fight back. It can only try to swim away. Why can't manatees fight enemies?

Gentle Giants

In some ways, a manatee's life is easy. A manatee is so big that alligators, crocodiles, and sharks usually leave it alone. It doesn't fight with other manatees over food or space. A manatee couldn't fight even if it wanted to. Its teeth are too far back in its mouth for it to bite an enemy. And its flippers aren't strong enough to hit hard.

Manatees aren't dangerous, and they move slowly. So it is easy for people to hunt manatees. Long ago, people in Florida hunted manatees for food. These people used manatee skin to make shields and shoes. People in some parts of the world still kill and eat manatees.

This man is reaching into a manatee's mouth to feed it. He knows the manatee will not bite him. Manatees bite only plants.

Even if a manatee sees a boat coming toward it, the manatee may not have time to swim out of the way.

In Florida, it is against the law to hunt manatees. But Florida manatees still have problems with people. Sometimes manatees rest near the water's surface. It is hard to see a resting manatee from a moving boat. So boats often hit manatees. A speeding motorboat can knock a manatee out. And the boat's spinning propeller may cut the manatee's body.

This manatee is sleeping at the bottom of a river. But sometimes manatees rest near the surface.

The scars on this manatee's back were made by a boat's propeller. Many manatees have propeller scars.

Humans also hurt manatees in other ways. Rain washes chemicals (KEH-mih-kuhlz) from factories and farms into the water where manatees live. Some of the chemicals kill underwater plants. Then manatees don't have enough to eat. Sometimes people leave fishhooks in the water. Manatees may die if they swallow the fishhooks. And some of the places where manatees once lived are gone. People filled these wet places with dirt to make dry land for houses.

Rain washes chemicals from the land into the water. Some of the chemicals hurt plants and animals who live in the water.

There are places in Florida where people help sick or hurt manatees. This woman is feeding a manatee at the Miami Seaquarium.

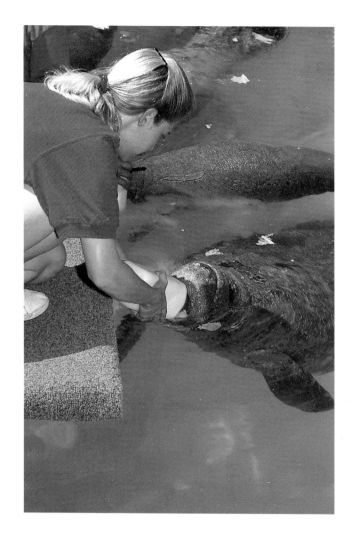

Once there were many thousands of Florida manatees. Only about 2,000 are left. That may seem like a lot. But Florida's coast is over 1,000 miles long. There is room for many more than 2,000 manatees.

Manatee cows don't have many calves. If too many manatees die, there may not be enough young manatees to take their places. The manatee might become extinct. When an animal is extinct, there are none left on earth. The manatee is endangered. That means it is in danger of becoming extinct.

One manatee lived for 35 years after people caught it.
No one knows how long wild manatees live.

Chapter 7

About 35 Florida manatees are killed by boats each year. How are people trying to protect manatees?

Human Friends

Every year, more people move to Florida. And more boats speed across Florida's waters. So Florida manatees are in great danger.

The people of Florida are trying hard to save their manatees. In many of the places where manatees live, it is against the law for boats to go fast. If boats go slowly, their drivers may see manatees. Then the boats won't run into the manatees. If a slowly moving boat does hit a manatee, the manatee may not be badly hurt.

Many manatees live in the Crystal River in Florida. This sign warns people in boats to watch out for manatees.

If you want to see wild manatees, visit Florida in the winter. Go to a warm water spring on a cool morning. You can watch manatees rest and play. A manatee may even let you rub and scratch it. Manatees seem to enjoy this.

Some manatees like to be scratched and petted.

People in Florida have set aside places where manatees are protected. This manatee is in Homosassa Springs State Wildlife Park. The park is a safe place for manatees.

By afternoon the manatees are hungry. They leave to find food. Their big tails move up and down slowly, as if to say good-bye. One by one, they disappear into the quiet, green water.

On Sharing a Book

As you know, adults greatly influence a child's attitude toward reading. When a child sees you read, or when you share a book with a child, you're sending a message that reading is important. Show the child that reading a book together is important to you. Find a comfortable, quiet place. Turn off the television and limit other distractions, such as telephone calls.

Be prepared to start slowly. Take turns reading parts of this book. Stop and talk about what you're reading. Talk about the photographs. You may find that much of the shared time is spent discussing just a few pages. This discussion time is valuable for both of you, so don't move through the book too quickly. If the child begins to lose interest, stop reading. Continue sharing the book at another time. When you do pick up the book again, be sure to revisit the parts you have already read. Most importantly, enjoy the book!

Be a Vocabulary Detective

You will find a word list on page 5. Words selected for this list are important to the understanding of the topic of this book. Encourage the child to be a word detective and search for the words as you read the book together. Talk about what the words mean and how they are used in the sentence. Do any of these words have more than one meaning? You will find these words defined in a glossary on page 46.

What about Questions?

Use questions to make sure the child understands the information in this book. Here are some suggestions:

> What did this paragraph tell us? What does this picture show? What do you think we'll learn about next? How are manatees like elephants? How are they different? Where do manatees live? How fast can manatees swim? What do manatees eat? How does a manatee clean its teeth? How long does a baby manatee stay with its mother? Why do boats often hit manatees? What do you think it's like being a manatee? What is your favorite part of the book? Why?

If the child has questions, don't hesitate to respond with questions of your own, such as: What do *you* think? Why? What is it that you don't know? If the child can't remember certain facts, turn to the index.

Introducing the Index

The index is an important learning tool. It helps readers get information quickly without searching throughout the whole book. Turn to the index on page 48. Choose an entry, such as *swimming,* and ask the child to use the index to find out how fast a manatee can swim. Repeat this exercise with as many entries as you like. Ask the child to point out the differences between an index and a glossary. (The index helps readers find information quickly, while the glossary tells readers what words mean.)

Where in the World?

Many plants and animals found in the Early Bird Nature Books series live in parts of the world other than the United States. Encourage the child to find the places mentioned in this book on a world map or globe. Take time to talk about climate, terrain, and how you might live in such places.

All the World in Metric!

Although our monetary system is in metric units (based on multiples of 10), the United States is one of the few countries in the world that does not use the metric system of measurement. Here are some conversion activities you and the child can do using a calculator:

WHEN YOU KNOW:	MULTIPLY BY:	TO FIND:
miles	1.609	kilometers
feet	0.3048	meters
inches	2.54	centimeters
gallons	3.787	liters
tons	0.907	metric tons
pounds	0.454	kilograms

Activities

Make up a story about manatees. Be sure to include information from this book. Draw or paint pictures to illustrate your story.

Manatees are in a group of animals called the Sirenia. The Sirenia are named after the sirens in Greek mythology. Go to the library and find out about the sirens.

Visit a zoo to see seals, dolphins, and other mammals who live in the water. How are manatees similar to these animals and how are they different?

Glossary

bulls—male manatees

calves—baby manatees

cows—female manatees

endangered—only a few of a kind of animal are still living

extinct—no members of a kind of animal are still living

graze—to eat plants

herbivores (HUR-buh-vorz)—animals who eat mostly plants

mammals—animals who are born alive and drink their mother's milk

nursing—drinking mother's milk

snout—the front part of an animal's head, including the nose, mouth, and jaws

springs—places where water comes out of the ground

streamlined—smooth and round. A streamlined body moves through water easily.

Index

Pages listed in **bold** type refer to photographs.